"The practical principles laid out in this book have been responsible for turning my business around over the last 12 months. My advice, take every word as gold and then implement. You'll be glad you did."

- Chris Perks (Digital Agency Owner & Founder of The Fast Growth Lab www.fastgrowthlab.com)

"Charlie & Emma have literally eliminated the frustration in explaining great ways to get more customers to say YES!"

- Samuel Leeds (Serial Entrepreneur, Bestselling Author & International Speaker www.Samuelleeds.com)

"A few months back, we were in a place where things were tough. The customers we were attracting were paying pittance for the work we were delivering. It was getting to the point where something had to give. Fortunately I spoke with Charlie. On the back of that conversation we implemented just one of the strategies outlined in this book. The net result was that within a few short days we'd landed a new client worth £24,000. The best part was we'd pitched at a price that we would have never dreamed of before - it was fantastic, and we have no one else but Charlie to thank!"

- Osmond Maguire (Owner and Director of WT Designs wtdesigns.co.uk)

THE
ORGASM
EFFECT

The Business Owners Guide to Get Customers Screaming

...Yes, Yes, **YES!**

CHARLIE HUTTON & EMMA HUTCHINSON

**Don't Forget To Watch The BONUS 4-Part
Documentary Series For Free!**

Finally *TRANSFORM* Your Business Into "**One Man Empire**" Without Being Held Hostage By An Army of Employees, By Watching This Ground Breaking Documentary Series...

All you have to do is go here now:

www.theonemanempire.com/documentary-fb/

LEGAL NOTICES

The Orgasm Effect: The Business Owners Guide To Get Customers Screaming, Yes, Yes YES!

Charlie Hutton &
Emma Hutchinson

Psst… Here's the secret to getting the most from this book. Don't put it down until you've gone through the whole enchilada.

Along the way you'll uncover a library of strategies taken from the real world. Strategies that time and time again have been proven to be a slam dunk by countless small business owners and entrepreneurs that have been transformed by just "trying" one or two things.

TABLE OF CONTENTS

A Word of Warning

This book is for business owners. Hopefully the title gave you a pretty big clue.

You could be a super successful business with a team of thousands, you could be an entrepreneur that is in the attempt of scaling up, you could be in your first year trading, or you could be just dipping your toe in the water of the entrepreneurial world.

It doesn't matter. As long as you have the entrepreneurial hunger to grow, this book can help you.

Business owners and entrepreneurs are the best people on the planet for two reasons:

1. You've got the drive

This book is a strategy. You have to implement it yourself. Having the drive to succeed means you get shit done. Do the activities outlined as 'making stuff happen' in the book and good stuff will happen. The value comes in implementing the strategy, not just reading about it.

2. You've got the mindset

The entrepreneurial outlook is rare. Its path involves risk and difficulty, but the entrepreneur is comfy with a level of risk. You know risk is the price to pay for success. You don't need stability of employment. You want to control your own path.

Like every strategy, the strategies within this book come with an element of risk. Some more than others. All we ask is that you to invest a little bit of money, and more importantly, some of your precious time into the things outlined.

There are two opposed ways of thinking when it comes to business. There's 'employee thinking' and 'entrepreneurial thinking'.

Employee thinking is narrow-minded. For example, lawyers are lawyers. Bakers are bakers. And so on and so on. That means they spend the lion's share of their time doing the thing that they are good at. But, this narrow-mindedness happens at the cost of everything else that needs to be done in their business.

Entrepreneurs however, build businesses. They look further and wider. They understand that they are in the business of marketing their business. They know to be a successful and profitable business owner they must acknowledge marketing and advertising. They know their number one job every single day is attracting customers.

If these traits don't describe you, we don't want to waste your time. It's probably best you use this book as a doorstop.

Oh, and there is a third reason. We get you. We understand you. Why? Because we are you.

What You Can Expect

I f you've been sitting on the fence trying to figure out how you get more paying customers into your business, then the fact that massive success is closer now than it's ever been, should have you salivating with excitement.

The current state of the global economy is the perfect storm for business owners who are nimble and willing to ride the wave. However, taking advantage of this new economy comes with one requirement:

You must take action now.

No more stalling, no more procrastination, no more day-dreaming about what it will feel like once you have a business that runs smoothly and successfully without you. No longer can you straddle the fence, waiting and hoping that a miracle cure will show up to magically solve all your problems.

What you hold before you is the ultimate step-by-step blueprint. It will take you by the hand and guide you through the danger riddled, but rewarding, journey of setting up a seven-step framework to driving a swarm of hungry customers to your door. No stone has been left unturned in providing you with a proven, tried and tested battle plan for lighting a rocket under your business.

We have included the information you will want to know in order to effectively market your business. More importantly, we have included the information that you will NEED to know to avoid getting ripped off, losing your sanity or giving up on your dream.

This book is unique in three major ways:

1. This book is meant to be used as your personal guide to effectively out market your competitors. A paint by numbers, fill in the blanks approach to successfully ratcheting your business to the next level.

2. This book prepares you to become an expert at attracting profitable prospects on demand: Your battle hardened plan to a steady flow of certain customers. Nothing has been left out.

3. This book breaks down all the vital parts of creating a successful marketing system that gets RESPONSE. It gives you the bird's-eye view and then swoops down for the kill, giving you an in-the-trenches inspection of each piece of the formula, so you can get your prospects to choose you.

As part of our journey together, you'll uncover:

- How to pinpoint and strengthen the parts of your sales funnel that will build epic amounts of goodwill and a lasting impression with every customer you meet.

- The deadly mistake that too many people make when trying to get customers that all but guarantees they say "no". If you only implement one thing, make sure it's this.

- Why the so-called "experts" are dead wrong in their ridiculous theories of "rapport" - Here's how you can create a powerful, instant connection with a customer by doing the exact opposite of what's "logical".

Plus much, much more.

By investing in this book, you've opened the door to an entire library about marketing your business that will serve as a guiding light of inspiration, encouragement, and sometimes an occasional kick up the arse.

That said, this book will not do the work for you. To really kick your business into high gear, you'll still need to add one simple ingredient.

IMPLEMENTATION.

We've even tried to shortcut that for you in the form of the 'making it happen' exercises, that you'll find dotted throughout the chapters in this book. Make sure you do them. There is no replacement for a strong will. You've already successfully overcome the first hurdle by grabbing a copy of this book, so don't fall at the next one by failing to take action and implement. Grab a pen, fill in the exercises and by the time you put this down you will have your very own framework for success.

That all said, let's leave you with some wise words from the legend that is Peter Drucker:

"Nothing happens until something gets sold!"

So go ahead, read this book cover to cover, make notes, fill in the exercises, implement and then sell something!

Ready to get cracking?

Great. Read on.

CHAPTER 1

Developing The Mindset For Massive Success

How To Remove That Niggling Doubt That's Been Holding You Back Since Day Dot...

T he fact of the matter is that in order for you to have any level of success with the strategies discussed in this book, you've first got to embrace the same mindset, beliefs, habits and goals of the entrepreneurial elite.

The harsh reality is that without the right mindset, you're destined to fail.

There is no magic pill.
There is no silver bullet.
There is no implement-in-five-minute solution.

We can't overcome your poor habits, lack of discipline and self-doubt for you. You have to.

If you're serious about success, then your real foundation, the true starting point, is addressing what's going on between your ears – what you believe, what your habits are and what goals you set.

These Are Your True Business Success Ingredients

There are three major ingredients that you need to have in order to turn your business around and become truly successful:

1. You must **think** like a member of the entrepreneurial elite.
2. You must **set goals** like the entrepreneurial elite.
3. You must **model** the systems of the entrepreneurial elite.

Success Ingredient #1 – What You Think

Anything you do in life starts with a simple thought. Therefore every breakthrough and success you'll ever have in your business will start with a simple thought. Thoughts are the seeds that grow into sales, profits and revenues.

Only if you can change the way you think, can you change your life and your business. You need to guard your mind against anything that will ruin the chances of your business and your strategy like your life depended on it, because it does. Never be passive about what you're reading, what you're watching or what you're listening to. You must be vigilant. Always be vigilant.

Entrepreneurial Elite Mindset Difference #1

The entrepreneurial elite are always thinking about the ways they can charge higher prices for a premium experience. Constantly brainstorming ways that they can offer top end experiences, products and value so that they feel justified in charging premium prices.

Instead of competing on price, their focus is on quality; quality products and quality services at a premium price. Only a premium service deserves a premium reward. You have to make your business look and act the part.

Though the entrepreneurial elite are sensitive to their customers' desire for a good deal and value, remember that people choose businesses, services and products for many other reasons besides the price.

The entrepreneurs elite realise that no matter how little they charge, someone can always charge less, so they don't play the lowest price game and neither should you.

Entrepreneurial Elite Mindset Difference #2

The entrepreneurial elite think about the habits they need to develop in order to accomplish their big goals. The truth of the matter is that your habits will either serve as a springboard to your next level of your success or serve as the quicksand that keeps you stuck at your current level, even sucking you further down.

These successful habits include things like:

- Attending marketing and personal development conferences on a regular basis.

- Investing in 1:1 coaching with experts and reading business improvement books on a regular basis.

- Weekly tracking and reviewing goals.

Entrepreneurial Elite Mindset Difference #3

The entrepreneurial elite read, watch and listen to things that support their belief that success is truly possible in every area of their business. They surround themselves with confidence and possibility. It's a proven fact that if you truly believe something is possible, you tend to focus on the ways to make that possibility a reality.

If you don't think something is do'able, then you'll tend to focus on why it can't be done. There are three stages of possibility that people can either get stuck in or develop through:

1. Thinking nothing is possible no matter what they do.
2. Thinking that something is possible.
3. Thinking that anything is possible.

So, here's the question you need to ask yourself...

"When presented with a challenge, do I first think of the ways I could succeed or the ways I could fail?"

The entrepreneurial elite are always looking for ways to get to the level of success that they envision in their mind.

The only real question for successful business owners is what they must change or do to get to the next level of success. Ask yourself: Is that how you view your business?

Entrepreneurial Elite Mindset Difference #4

The entrepreneurial elite know that they'll never be successful if they're always stuck doing grunt work. The top business owners have a specific view of their role as the owner and what they should and should not be doing in their businesses.

They spend their time developing new marketing campaigns, creating new lines of business and adapting to constantly changing local market conditions. They know the value of creating systems and focusing on income-producing activities.

Entrepreneurial Elite Mindset Difference #5

The entrepreneurial elite move forward with good plans and marketing strategies even if they're afraid. One of the big obstacles for most entrepreneurs is that they take one or more steps forward, but because they hit a few roadblocks or issues along the way, they stop and become paralyzed by the fear of failing.

When most feel that fear, they tend to give in. They lose all the momentum they've gained. What they should do is reflect on what's truly going on in their heart and mind, and the market itself, which is exactly what the successful business owner does.

Some successful entrepreneurs are even able to use this fear of failure to motivate themselves to take massive action instead of being frozen solid. See fear as an opportunity.

Success Ingredient #2 – Your Goals

Now that you have set your mind, clarified your thinking, and strengthened your beliefs, it's time to know and set your goals. The entrepreneurial elite **sets goals** for their business by answering one question.

That question is very simple...

Where Are You Headed?

Many business owners float aimlessly from one cash crisis to the next, which is a terrible way to run any business and an even worse way to live. You need to set daily, weekly and monthly goals. These smaller goals, will serve as your road map to your BIG business goals and aspirations.

Do You Have Big Goals For Your Business?

Tiny goals equal tiny results.

I see tiny goal setting all the time. Does this sound familiar?

You settle for having a quiet period on Thursday, and then Fridays too. You just end up trying to cover your overheads and hope you have a little bit left at the end. You take most of that little bit that's left over and use it to try and prove to your spouse that things are okay.

I was at a regional business event last week and saw a prime example of tiny goals. Stand after stand of small business owners stood eagerly behind a table, each with a fishbowl, hoping to collect a few business cards from the day.

Small tiny goals, give you small tiny results.

So, how about some BIG goals that'll get you BIG results?

How about consistently filling your business with customers every day of the week? Aiming to attract 100-300 brand new customers, each and every month? Or maybe getting featured in national newspapers and press regularly?

You see, the fact is...

"You will become as small as your controlling desire; or as great as your dominant aspiration."

Don't be afraid to chase greatness.

The truth is that most great achievements in life are the result of thinking big and aiming high. Small goals put chains, restrictions and limits on your potential. When you're working towards a big goal you barrel right through tons of smaller ones by virtue of chasing that one big goal. Every journey must have a destination in mind.

Success Ingredient #3 – Modelling Success

Modelling the proven systems and processes of other successful businesses and entrepreneurs is the missing ingredient that most business owners are looking for. Imagine having the exact strategies, process and systems that other successful business owners have used to explode their profits and putting them to work for you.

It's all there waiting for you. I mean, they've done the hard work for you already – you just need to apply that work to your business.

The profits however, are not just in simply having the blueprints in your hand.

The real gold, the real profit, the real breakthrough, lies in your ability to actually implement those strategies - you don't need to re-invent the wheel.

Don't Reinvent The Wheel!

Don't fall for the classic mistake of thinking that you're the only one who doesn't have enough money for advertising or that you're the only one that's ever been muscled out by cheap online competitors.

You're not.

Every problem, every challenge you have in your business has already been faced and solved by other successful entrepreneurs. Look to them. Grasp their winning strategy and put into action in your business. The real issue is in finding the solution, but since you've invested in this book, you already have many of the answers you've been looking for.

The Power of Modelling

You have to start using blueprints or roadmaps by others. It will dramatically decrease the amount of time and money you waste. That's why it's so important that you attend conferences, events and invest in and coaching programs.

In his book "Unlimited Power", Tony Robbins wrote this about the power of modelling others success:

- Success leaves clues, the people who produce outstanding results do specific things to create those results.

- Modelling is the pathway to excellence… The movers and shakers of the world are often professional modellers—people who have mastered the art of learning everything they can by following other people's experience rather than just relying on their own.

- To model excellence you should be a detective, an investigator, someone who asks lots of questions and tracks down all the clues to what produces that excellence. Building from the successes of others is one of the fundamental aspects of most learning.

With that in mind, even when you find a successful business system or process to model, you'll have a final hurdle to overcome…

The Hidden Pitfall of Modelling

The irony is that when most struggling business owners get to peek behind the curtain of what successful businesses do, they're quickly bored and unimpressed with the proven systems and processes that multi-million pound businesses are using.

They often complain that it seems too simple and easy.

They can't get their heads around how simple it can be to achieve massive success. So, they carry on doing what they're doing and either never attempt the strategy in the first place or make it so complicated for themselves that they give up before they started.

Success is not complicated. It's often the simple, un-sexy, boring strategies that can have the biggest impact on your bottom line.

The Hidden Path to Success

Don't incorrectly think that the road to success is hidden away. Don't think that if you could find it, it would be a twisting, uphill battle, covered in fog and full of pitfalls.

- **Don't** distrust obvious and straight forward answers your problems.

- **Don't** complicate simple concepts because you think the truth is "common sense."

- **Don't** gravitate towards the secretive and mysterious because you believe that they hold magical alluring qualities.

Model Your Way to Success

Successful business owners know that their success is dependent on their ability to discover the simple but powerful things that they can leverage to consistently grow their business. They know that the more complicated it is, the less likely they and their staff will be able to implement it consistently.

No matter how simple it looks, they do it and test the results. You need to do the same for yourself. Let's face it, the wheel is far from complicated, but it revolutionized the world.

CHAPTER 2

Marketing That Will Make You Money

How To Get A 2 For 1 Return On Any Marketing Spend, In Any Market...

I t's time to face the music, the market's changed. The taste and expectations of customers have changed. The economy has changed. The question is,

"Why haven't you changed?"

The Old Way:

If you're a slave to your business and you're working 14-18 hours a day, you're doing things the old way. The wrong way. If you're forced to submit to the whim of every Tom, Dick and Harry that comes into your business because you're desperate for money, you haven't changed and you're doing things the old way.

If you try to sell anything and everything that you can because you're trying to be a one-stop shop business, you're doing things the old way. If you're wasting tons of money on image ads that brag about how great your business is, you're doing things the old way.

The New Way:

- You're in the new era if there are new customers "finding" your business every day online. Technology has evolved and so has business. You should too.

- You have developed a way of learning exactly what ad or marketing effort generated every customer who visits your business. Finding what works to attract is vital in attracting even more success.

- You are collecting your customer's contact information so you can notify them of your offers and build greater long term goodwill. Loyalty and momentum go a long way.

It's about enjoying your life and having greater peace of mind knowing you have leveraged the best system to help you get the best possible result.

The One Thing

What's the one thing that will determine whether or not your business succeeds? Is it product quality? Is it customer service? Or is it good staff & support team? Is it because you have the lowest prices on the block or the best location in town?

WRONG!

Your ability to consistently attract new customers and convert them into loyal customers, is the number one determinant of your real business success. In other words MARKETING!

The Secret to Success

The sooner you become the marketer of your business instead of the doer of your business, the faster your income and business will grow!

What Is The New Definition of Marketing?

Marketing is anything that you would do or can do to get customers AND keep customers. Period.

Everything is marketing... and marketing is everything to your success.

ALL marketing strategies MUST be held accountable to produce profits. This means that you must know the effectiveness of each advert, voucher, letter, flyer, postcard, blog post and even tweet.

Your goal is to create a marketing system that's predictable and repeatable. In order to reach that goal, you should be able to know the exact thing that brought every customer into your business.

The Two Types of Marketing Strategies.

Strategy #1: Mass or Brand Marketing - the stuff you see everywhere. Unless you have been living without access to any media (and if so how did you get a copy of this book?!) you'll see mass image focused marketing across the TV, radio, print and the internet on a minute by minute basis.

The goal of this type of marketing is to remind customers and prospects about you and your brand, and the products that you offer. The dons of this are the big boys – Apple, John Lewis, Tesco. They've got this bad boy nailed.

Mass marketing gets a bad rep. Anyone that tells you that this stuff, when it's done well, doesn't work, are either fibbing or never tried it on scale.

This marketing is effective, but it is expensive. It takes money and it takes time. The idea is that the more times you run ads from your brand, the more likely people are to have this brand at the top of their consciousness when they go to make a purchase. You've got to run your marketing A LOT to let it sink into people. It'll be there in their subconscious, waiting, even when they don't know it.

The vast majority of marketing falls into this category, especially in the corporate world. The expense and time involved are not a problem for the big corporates as they have mega budgets. Whole teams and contractors are dedicated to this stuff, because it works.

But (and it's a big but), if you can't invest the money and the time this type marketing will fail EVERYTIME. This is exactly why it's not the best fit for the small business.

Most simply don't have the budget to run ads in sufficient volume to make them effective. It's why the vast majority of small businesses that try this kind of approach will never see a return on their investment.

Fortunately there is an answer.

Strategy #2: Direct Response

Here is the all-knowledgeable Google's definition of the word 'response':

Response: noun - A reaction to something

This perfectly sums up what you're aiming to do with a direct response lead campaign – get a reaction. In other words, the use of media (marketing efforts) to get people to respond to your messages, pick up the phone, make a purchase, fill a form out online – DO STUFF – that you want them to do.

When it comes to direct response, the goal is that every pound you spend must come back to your bank account with at least two new friends to joining him. That's a £2 return for £1 invested. Doubling your investment.

For the small mighty businesses and entrepreneurial elite, a direct response style of approach to getting customers is 'the holy grail' – here's why:

1) It's about your customers: This works because direct response marketing is all about your customers, not you! Brand marketing does exactly what it says on the tin - and is focused on the brand that is doing the marketing. Direct response, however, is all about the customer. It talks to the customers about their interests, desires, fears and frustrations. It compels them to take action by taking a stronger interest.

2) It's track-able: That is, when someone responds, you know exactly where it came from, which channel, which media and which piece of content was responsible for generating the response. This is in direct contrast to brand led marketing – no one will ever know what ad compelled you to buy that can of Coke, heck you may not even know yourself!

3) It's targeted: Direct marketing by its nature is very, very targeted. It focuses on getting a response from a specific audience, your ideal customers. You are aiming to appeal to a defined audience, one which is profitable.

4) It's measurable: Since you know what your customers are responding to, you can measure the effectiveness of every campaign you're doing.

5) It's controllable: Since direct response marketing is targeted, track-able, and measurable, you're the one with ultimate control. And this is your dream scenario – because it allows you to max out your return on investment. This means you can keep improving your marketing, scale up anything that's a winner and trash any duds quickly.

When done correctly, there is no better investment in your business than marketing. Everything else is a cost. You must know your return on investment (ROI) at all times by using direct response marketing. Keep it simple. Keep it profitable.

CHAPTER 3

Getting Clarity On WTF You're Really Doing

The 3 Things You Absolutely MUST Know To Grow...

U nless you've been living under a rock, you've probably noticed that the economy has changed. Attracting new customers and keeping your existing customers happy might be harder than ever before.

It can be tough out there, but why is it so much harder to get more customers for your business now, than it was? Well, it's because you've probably not got a solid understanding of what you're really doing in your business:

- What the hell you *really* selling?
- Who the hell are you *really* selling it too?

- How much money they *really* making you?

At first glance they might seem kind of obvious, but it's with these three elements that the battle is won or lost. As we dive into each, experience would tell us that you'll be surprised how little you know the answers to each of the above.

Success Fundamental #1: What The Hell Are You Really Selling?

Under no circumstances should you be selling your services - EVER. Sounds odd I know, but read on.

By simply selling what you do (accountancy, personal training, financial advice, marketing, graphic design etc.) you open up to be compared to everyone else in your marketplace on apples for apples basis. It's a bad place to be as it results in a constant battle on price.

Instead you need to sell the transformation that your services offer - the sizzle not the steak.

Demonstrating Results In Advance

The best way to get a handle on what you're really selling is by using a "Results in Advanced Timeline" – something conceived by Internet marketing guru Frank Kern. We've adapted the process slightly but here's how it starts:

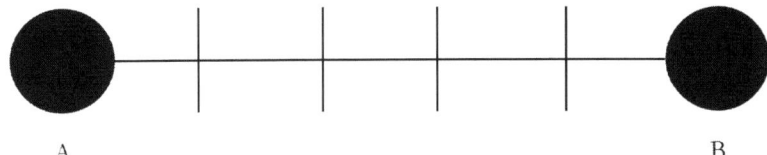

A   B

It represents your customers' journey from where they are right now (point A) to get to where they need to be (point B) and the four or five major milestones (the vertical lines) they need to overcome on the way.

Whatever your business is, whatever the transformation is that you take people through, just work out the four or five major steps that need to happen to get your customers and you from A to B.

Let's look at an example.

Example: Personal Trainer

Underneath Point A you'd write. "Overweight", because that's where a new customer starts.

And then under Point B you'd write beach body – in other words, where they want to be. If we were targeting males, they'd probably want that elusive six pack that they can proudly parade around the beach.

Let's then think about how someone might go from overweight to a beach body.

Milestone #1: Understanding they have a problem. They need educating as to why there are overweight and why they've got a problem. So they need to come to a realisation.

A conclusion along the lines of:

"You know what? I'm overweight. There is a reason why I'm overweight - I eat more calories than I burn."

Milestone #2: Counting or "controlling calories", AKA an understanding of what needs to be eaten on a daily basis.

Milestone #3: Exercising to burn off excess calories and tone muscles.

Milestone #4: "Lifestyle". The making sure and understanding that calorie control and exercise need to be a regular part of their day-to-day living.

This leaves you with a diagram like the one below.

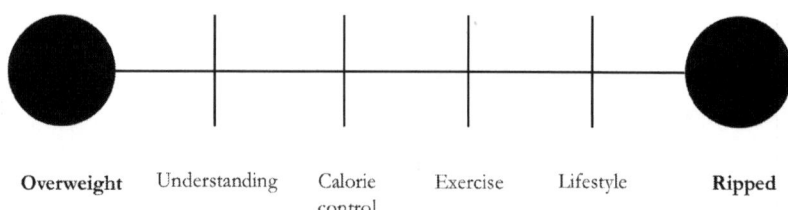

Overweight   Understanding   Calorie control   Exercise   Lifestyle   **Ripped**

Example: Financial Advisor

Under Point A, a starting point could be "Not Saving Enough" or "Struggling with Finances" with the end goal, Point B, being "Retirement at a Beach".

Leaving the five milestones as:

Milestone #1: An understanding of current finances.

Milestone #2: Calculating a monthly saving plan.

Milestone #3: Establishing how to save that monthly magic number.

Milestone #4: Automation – setting up regular direct debits and transfers so it happens without thinking about it.

You get the idea.

Showcasing the Big Payoff

With a true understanding of the transformation in place, the magic finally happens. These milestones are not only about getting your customers to their ideal goal. They are also the foundations of your brand, because you have a system and process you can now name, which is loaded with benefits.

This name needs to showcase the big payoff that your transformation will deliver.

Let's go back to the personal trainer example. The name could be:

"Buffed Body Boot Camp - 90 Day Transformation Training Programme."

Notice by giving it a brand and calling it something, it instantly becomes benefit driven. Plus, it separates you from everyone else in your marketplace, even though in principle you're selling much the same product. You've got to package those services uniquely.

Yes, your competitors might walk people through the exact same five steps, but they'll be selling the service, not 'the transformation'.

Because let's be clear, whatever you're selling people, they want the end result.

Having a branded system stops people comparing price and price alone because they can't compare apples for apples. Let's be honest – what would you choose:

A) Three months of personal sessions @ £397

OR

B) Buffed Body Boot Camp - 90 Day Transformation Training Programme @ £397

Probably (B) every time right?

Probably still even (B) if the price was maybe two or even three times as much!

Making Stuff Happen

EXERCISE #1:
Complete Your Results in Advanced Timeline

Fill in the blank framework below for your business:

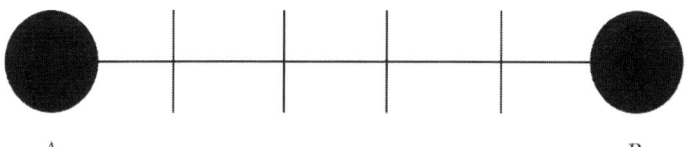

A   B

Choose the new "brand" name of transformation that showcases the big payoff?

Success Fundamental #2: Who The Hell Are You Really Selling To?

This part is really key. It will impact on everything you do in your business from here on in, so go over it a few times if you have to.

It's all about working out:
- Who you are selling to?
- Who your ideal customers are?
- What are they all about?
- And how can you appeal to them like no one else?

If a person is going to buy your products and services, it will pay you back ten-fold to really understand them. If you can find, and then pull, at their heart-strings, you can get them exactly where you want them.

In this part of the book we'll walk you through how to create Ideal Customer Profiles.

A customer profile is what should be at the forefront of your mind when you create ANY new campaign, product advert or marketing activity.

The good news is, putting these together is really easy.

Simply ask yourself, what makes someone the ideal customer for you? Note some things down. Depending on how big your business is, or how good you are at knowing and collecting data on your customers, you might not have all of this to hand, but don't let that stop you.

Make a guess if you have to, so that you can build the picture.

There are six vital elements to building a rock solid customer profile. Let's work through an example of one of our ideal customer profiles to show you what this looks like.

Example Ideal Customer

#1 : BACKGROUND

Name	Driven Daniel
Sex	Male
Age Range	30-45
Relationship	Married/partner
Children	Yes, primary aged
Location	Midlands, England
Education	Doesn't matter
Job Title	Managing Director, Founder, Owner
Industry	Professional services
Business Size	Under 20 employees
Turnover	£750,000 - £5m

#2 : HERO QUOTE — 'Make me money, and save me time by doing it for me'

#3 : VALUES
Self-made
Driven to grow and ambitious
Top of his own ladder
Wants to work with experts
Traditional family values

#4 : CHALLENGES   Working too many hours
Pulled in a lot of directions
Not an expert
Not enough time at home
Wants more free time
Wants to take business to next
level

#5 : INTERESTS   Executive tastes, home, car,
holidays
Enjoys things but is not flash
Conservative
Family time
Health conscious
Individual sports e.g. cycling

#6 : SOURCES

GOING TO   St Pauls Club, Lexicon, Henley,
Local races

READING   Entrepreneur, Success,
Minds in Business

LOOKS UP TO   Giants - Kennedy, Robbins, Sugar

The Background demographic is really important, despite it often being about your ideal customer's personal life and not their 'work life'. This helps you get inside their head... and think like them. This is the key to winning them as a new customer!

Use the Values section of your customer's profile to call out which of these you and your business appeal to. Pull these 'matches' out in your marketing and interactions so that your ideal prospects can identify with you. People like to buy from others who are just like them, it's a behavioural law.

Sources help when it comes to looking at where you will find these customers, such as where you could advertise, attend networking etc.

Use the 'but no one else would' trick when you are thinking of these so you can find niche details about your ideal customer. For example, in the cooking sector, everyone would know Jaime Oliver, but only those really into French cuisine would know Paul Bucose.

This is where you can really outsmart your competitors, as none of them will be thinking this tactically. Think outside of the box.

Also think about why would your ideal customer choose NOT to buy your product or service? These "objections" must be addressed in your marketing.

You can start by building a single customer profile. But don't stop there. Once you get the hang of it, you'll be churning out multiple profiles, which will represent the different parts of your market, as well as different and new products.

Now, over to you...

Making Stuff Happen

EXERCISE #2:
Build our own Ideal Customer Profile.

BACKGROUND
Name
Sex
Age Range
Relationship
Children
Location
Education
Job Title
Industry
Business
Turnover

HERO QUOTE

VALUES

CHALLENGES

INTERESTS

SOURCES
Going To
Reading

Success Fundamental #3: How Much Money Are They *Really* Making You?

Let's now talk about the most important number you need to know in order to scale and grow your business – the "Life Time Value of a Customer."

Life Time Value is *"On average, how much a customer is likely to spend with your business over a given period of time."*

Understanding exactly how much a customer is worth to your business allows you to know exactly how much you can spend to bring a new customer through the door. In order to calculate the lifetime value of your customers, you need to know answers to the following questions:

- Your Average Sale Per Person
- Number of Visits Per Month/Year
- Sales Per Customer Per Year
- Average Number Of People Per Table
- Number of Referrals Per Customer
- Average Number of Years A Customer Stays

If you don't know the answers to these questions then you are at a HUGE disadvantage – so go find them out!

Here is an example:

Your Average Sale Per Person   £35
Number of Sales Per Year   10
Average Number of Years Customer Stays   5

The Calculation (Multiple Them Together)

£35 x 10 per year x 5 years = Life Time Value

Life Time Vale Of Customer (5 years)   £1,750

In this example, if you knew each and every single customer, over their lifetime, is going to spend £1,750 with you, would you be willing to spend £5, £50, possibly even £500, to acquire that customer?

Your answer should be a YES, YES, YES.

It's a no brainer – because it's literally just trading in money for something higher in return. Consider it the act of purchasing customers.

Your Life Time Customer Value number is an especially useful tool when it comes to attracting premium clients. It allows you to spend more on marketing to make sure that you attract the right sort of people in.

Once we know what that average spend is, we need to know, on average, have many times and what they will purchase per month.

We can then take this one step further by taking into consideration that satisfied customers will also refer people – if incentivised in the right way. So if we go back to the example, and presumably each happy customer will refer just three people over their lifetime, it means on top of the customers lifetime value we also now have:

Number of Referrals Per Customer   3
Gross Sales For Total Referrals (5 years)   £5,250

There. The total value of a satisfied customers is now
£7,000.

Knowing this number is the quickest way to take over
any market. It allows you to outspend every single
competitor in your market to get a customer to buy from
you and not them.

Total Value Of 10 Happy Customers   £70,000
Total Value Of 100 Happy Customers   £700,000
Total Value Of 1000 Happy Customers   £7,000,000

Most businesses have more than enough customers in
their target market to build a 7-figure business easily.
However, they do little to nothing to get people to come
back and refer others, and that's where the problem is.

Making Stuff Happen

EXERCISE #3:
Calculating Your Life Time Customer Value

Dig out your customers spending, or if you are new take an educated guess. Work out your Life Time Customer Value as above.

Your Average Sale Per Person:

Number of Sales Per Year:

Average Number of Years Customer Stays:

What can you afford to spend to acquire a customer?

CHAPTER 4

Establishing Undeniable Proof

The Deadly Mistake That Too Many People Make When Trying To Show Proof...

We live in an age of increasing scepticism and caution, which means your ability to prove what you do needs to be undeniable. No matter where you are, how long you've been in business, or how solid your positioning is you need to keep proving what you do. Constantly.

Even the massive entity that McDonald's is do it. They do it everywhere with one very simple statement:

"Over 90 Billion Served."

They're using a ridiculous number to back up some of the things that they say about their great-tasting burgers. After all, how could all ninety billion people be wrong?

That said, let's assume that you've not served ninety billion people, or that you don't have the budget of the Golden Arches, here's the next best thing:

Transformation Testimonials

People and businesses that have been through your transformation, have used your services, and gone from where they were to where they need to be.

I know testimonials are an idea as old as time. However, there is a right way and a wrong way to receive and present testimonials.

The Bad Testimonial – A Non Success Story

The bad testimonial covers the majority of all testimonials you'll ever hear, see or read – they look like this:

"Joe was great."

"Great job, Joe."

"Thanks, I'm going to use you guys again."

They all suck. They're generic and boring. They don't get you enthusiastic or overly excited about the company or the product.

They don't show a transformation.

The Good Testimonial – The Transformation

A good testimonial demonstrates a success STORY and delivers proof of your ability to deliver their desired transformation. It shows your customers undeniable proof that you are the greatest.

EXAMPLE – Transformational Testimonial

"I just wanted to take a minute and let you know how the Beach Buff personal training program I invested in from Chris has helped my confidence no end. Before I invested in the weekly one-on-one training sessions, I was dropping a few pounds a month, but it was like pulling teeth. After working with Chris for just 14 days I dropped more weight than I had in the last 3 months. By the time my summer holiday rolled round, my six-pack was the envy of everyone at the hotel."

How much more powerful is this over, "Chris is awesome" or "Chris did a great job in getting me fit"?

Let's deconstruct the highlights:

Highlight #1: It name drops the system – Beach Buff

Highlight #2: It uses the word invest – nice psychological trigger as it positions Beach Body as an investment, not a cost.

Highlight #3: It paints a picture of their state before meeting Chris.

Highlight #4: It then paints a picture of the end result – "my six-pack was the envy of everyone at the hotel."

Highlight #5: It clearly shows a journey (a transformation) from problem to solution.

Transformation Testimonial Extraction

Step #1 – Ask For It

Obvious I know, but when was the last time you asked for one?

Don't fall into the trap that just because you did a fantastic job that a customer will give you a testimonial out of the kindness of their heart.

The majority of people won't. People are busy, they have other stuff to do. You need to prompt. It doesn't matter how big of a transformation that you put them through, how much you've helped them solve their problems, you still need to make sure that you ask.

The best time to ask is while they are still hot. In other words, right after they got their first BIG result or overcame that first major milestone.

Step #2 – Show Them What To Do

Create a document or web page that shows your customers how to leave the perfect testimonial – on it include:

- What information they should to include in it.
- Give an example of a good testimonial.
- Give an example of a bad testimonial.
- Provide a fill in the blanks example – a cookie cutter customer time saver.
- Ask them to video it too.

Fill-In-The-Blanks Transformation Testimonial

I just want to take a minute and let you know how the
_____ I invested in
from_____ has helped my
_____.

Before I invested in _____, I felt
_____, _____and
_____.

However, after working with _____
I've noticed _____,
_____ and _____.
I just want to say _____.

Now you don't want to give everyone the same template because your testimonials will all look the same. But if you create 5 or 6 templates, tailored to your business, you'll be away at the races.

Step #3 – Collation

Collect your transformational testimonials into one document or book, whether that'd be digitally or in print, and start showcasing them – EVERYWHERE.

We worked with a great B2B company who put all of their testimonials in a big binder. Nothing fancy but it was BIG. Over the years, this binder has grown to six, all of which sit at the reception desk in the office, so anyone coming into the office for the first time see on this GIANT stack undeniable proof of the business's success and capability.

CHAPTER 5

Attracting Buyers Not Busters

How To All But Eliminate Every Single Time Waster & Freebie Seeker That Is Ever Likely to Plague Your Business...

Here's the thing you've got to do. Stop trying to attract anyone and everyone to your business. You should only focus on attracting your best type of customers. Dealing with timewasters, tyre kickers and freebie seekers are a drain on resources, energy and moral.

Banning the Word Free

Let's be clear. Using the word "free" in any marketing campaign will bump response dramatically, but let us ask you this question:

If you use the word "free" everywhere in your marketing and your messages, how can you then sit back and wonder why you only ever attract freebie seekers and timewasters?

Just ask yourself how many times you've heard the phase:

"I've just got no money right now – maybe next month."

Then ask yourself how these people first come into contact with your business. Free consultation? Free report or free guide? Chances are they did, and that is probably why they're so price sensitive. Now, don't panic. There are alternate ways to create incentives.

1) Simply change the word "free" to "complimentary".

Yes, it still means the same thing, but it doesn't necessarily quite have the same impact that "free" has in attracting those without money.

2) Create a **customer attraction magnet**.

Yes, that says customer NOT lead magnet!

Now the good news is this is easy to do. Instead of offering new people that come into contact with your business "freebies" make them a "No Brainer" offer that **they pay for**.

The goal here is to turn a possible new lead into a customer, even if it's a low-ticket customer. You want to give them a way in to spend some money fast, ideally in a way that is also going to demonstrate how good you are at what you do and why they should start considering your services or products when it comes to buying at higher prices. A good way to do this is to make sure that the thing offered gets them part way to the results or even solves an existing problem or minor gripe.

This not only provides a demonstration of power, but it more importantly allows you to build a list of customers. Let's be clear. We are generating a list of hot leads that are willing to put their hands in their pockets and spend money with you - buyers.

This hot lead or customer list will be the most valuable asset you will ever have in your business. Forget the phrase "the money is in the list," because the real money is in a qualified, engaged list of people who have already spent money with you.

What He-Man & The Masters Of The Universe Has To Do With You Attracting High Quality Buyers

Back in the 1980s, I (Charlie), like most kids, was a huge fan of He-Man and the Masters of the Universe.

At the time, I managed to persuade my parents to sign me up for the Masters of the Universe Club, which cost about £1.99. From what I remember, you'd sign up by sending in three stamps and a self-addressed envelope for full membership into the Club.

What a customer attraction magnet!

These guys were now exclusively talking to people that were really, really interested in He-Man – the members. This tactic separated those people that were just fans from those who were actually willing to spend money on this sort of thing.
They got people to make a low level purchase of £1.99 and then on a monthly basis, they'd send out a mini-catalogue with stories from Castle Grey Skull, insight into characters and, most important of all, offers. There was always an offer of the month. The promotions were based around buying bigger and better toys.

Guess what happened?

They sold toys. A lot of toys on a monthly basis. Each time a "member" got a catalogue, chances are they brought something – or got parents to!

The attract system here was great. It's one that's easily replicated. Simply create a mechanism to bring people into your world, and then quickly identify those that are actually willing to spend money.

They might be small time spenders at the start but, with the right follow up, these are the ones that will quickly buy again and again, because a buyer is a buyer is a buyer.

Bottom line, you need to create a low barrier to entry customer magnet to separate freebie seekers from spenders.

It makes sense to do it during your lead generation activities to save any hassles and wasted time with "dud" prospects down the line.

Customer Attraction Magnet Example #1:
99 cent Domains @ GoDaddy

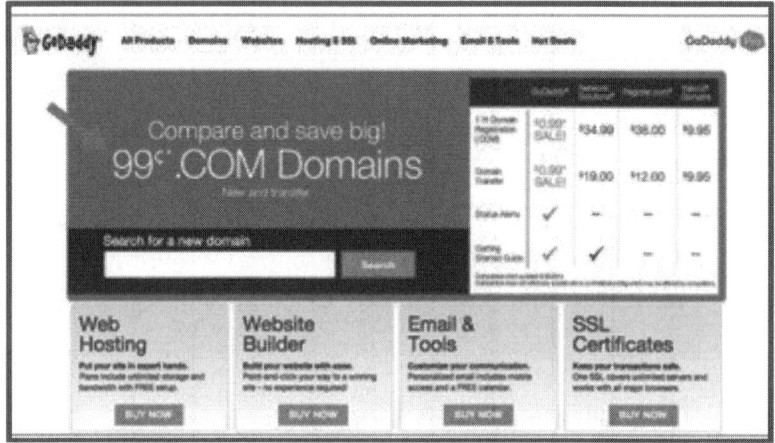

GoDaddy (godaddycom) are prolific with their use of customer magnets. Chances are you've probably even brought one and never even noticed it. You see their big offer at the front is 99 cent .com domains. It's a mechanism designed to turn browsers into customers - very quickly and very easily.

Now, they're a volume based business, but they know if somebody's going to buy a .com domain for $0.99, they're probably, going to buy some other things as well.

They're going to want some hosting; maybe email and renewals down the line. This offer gets the customers in the door, opens up their wallets and means GoDaddy is focusing on buyers. After all, GoDaddy could easily give these domains away for free as a loss leader on the front end, but they're smart enough to know the psychology involved in attracting people that commit to spending just a small amount of money and repelling freebie seekers in the process.

Customer Attraction Magnet Example #2: $1 Yoga Equipment @ Yoga Trapeze

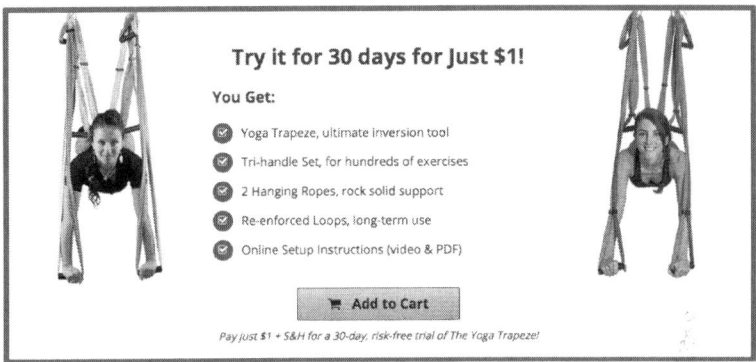

Yoga Body (yogabody.com) has a $200 piece of yoga equipment called the Yoga Trapeze. Now, rather than allowing people to try the equipment for free, they instead offer a $1 trial. You pay them $1 and they will let you try the Yoga Trapeze in your home for 30 days. If you like it you pay the balance, if you don't, well it goes back.

What's great about this is that once it's set up in the home and being used as part of a daily routine, how many people do you think want to send the thing back?

I'm guessing not very many. The net result is that customers open their wallets and prove that they're willing to spend money.

Customer Attraction Magnet Example #3:
$1 Book Offer @ GKIC.

Dan Kennedy and the team at GKIC (gkic.com) have used this lead generation strategy to great effect with multiple offerings, to build a huge list of buyers.

It's simple. Take a book, which has a real world value of about $12-20, and then give it away for just $1, including postage. What's smart about this kind of offer is that the advert clearly states that the book is going to cost you $1. Meaning that anyone clicking on the ad knows that they're about to be sold something.

When the book is purchased, a physical copy is sent out in the post along with an audio CD. Both do a great job of selling (without actually selling) the idea that GKIC and Dan Kennedy are experts in their field and should be listened to.

If you have written your own book, then this is a great offer to start with at the front end. At just $1, this is pretty much as close as you can get to a free offer, but at the same time it makes a prospect actually have to take out a credit card and commit to a purchase. As noted before, this filters out the majority of time-wasters and freebie seekers.

Customer Attraction Magnet Example #4: Exit Strategy Kit @ Walter Bergeron.

Walter Bergeron (walterbergeron.com) helps business owners plan for the best ways to exit and sell their business. Rather than try to sell his services from his website, Walter offers visitors his "Exit Strategy Business Sales Kit." He puts a whole host of information in a box and ships a physical package out to the customer at just a small cost (to the customer) of $12.65.

Let's be clear. $12.95 is just a drop in the pond compared to what his consulting services go for. This investment becomes a no brainer if it means a business owner can add an extra couple of zeros to the sale price.

Like Yoga Trapeze, Walter is sending a physical item in the post. Something that his prospects can hold and feel, something that is going to demonstrate that Walter knows what he says is knows. It instantly positions him as an expert and authority in the market.

The good news for Walter is that he can now focus his marketing efforts on the list of people that have raised their hands and have demonstrated that they are willing to invest money to help solve this problem.

This is a great example of how to apply this principle at the top of a sales funnel for high ticket consulting services. Even if a loss is made on the front end, the Life Time Value of a customer makes this type of approach very scalable.

<u>Customer Attraction Magnet Example #5:</u>
£99 Video Business Card @ Bear Kap.

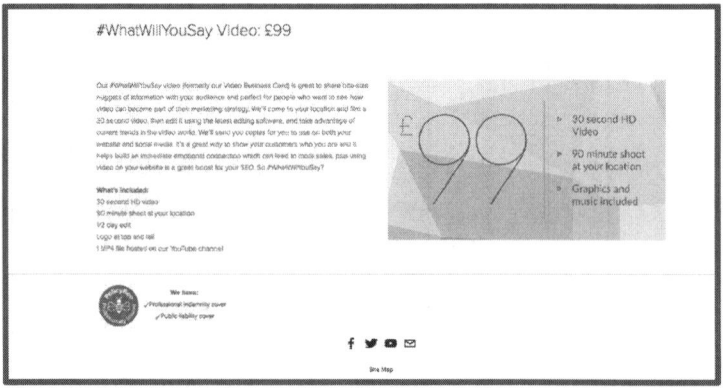

Yes, this can also be done in person!

A good friend of ours, Benjamin Kalsi, runs a local videographer company – Bear Kap (bearkap.co.uk). Benjamin's premium services start from £2,000 upwards but due to the competition in the marketplace – negotiation on price is rife.

So here's what Benjamin pitches when he goes to networking events as a customer magnet.

A 30 seconds HD video of you talking to camera for only £99.

He gets 99 quid in his back pocket, which, let's be honest, isn't gonna set the world alight, but probably covers petrol and minor expenses.

It does however mean Benjamin's acquired a new customer, one that is willing to spend money. What do you think happens when they see how the video looks, see how well it's recorded and Benjamin's professionalism? Well most of them get him to do a bunch of other stuff too at a premium rate, one that is never haggled on because they're already seen the value in his work and now don't want to go elsewhere.

The cherry on the cake

Now the real advantage of customer magnets over a typical "freebie" lead magnet is this. What do you do every time you spend money online? Well you give your REAL email address, the one you check all the time, not the 'test@test.com' we're all guilty of using to access the odd free report or voucher from time to time.

This means that you're not only attracting buyers, but you're also building a list of good quality clean data.

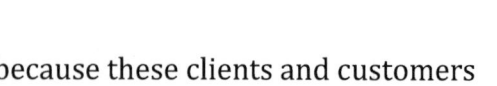

Which of course, because these clients and customers are spending money, will also consist of a mailing address and phone number. It's what we call a win win.

Places to look for inspiration

A great place to start looking for ideas is Fiverr. Go have a look on fiverr.com and see what kind of services people are offering for $5.00. It will give you an idea of what your business can offer. It can open up your thinking too, "You know what? If these guys can do it for $5.00, we could too." Or of course you could just pay them to do it for you!

More Inspiration – Paul the Fitness Coach

Paul is in the fitness coaching market. He coaches people on how to improve their fitness. His customer attraction magnets could include:

- A 10 Minute Body Blitz for £10.00.

- A FREE pedometer – just pay postage. Something that could be sourced from China and shipped out less than £5.

- A £55 full body fitness assessment.

More Inspiration – Steve the Financial Advisor

Steve advises people how to best plan for retirement and manage money in the short and long term. His customer attraction magnets could include:

- A £15 cash flow credit check report.

- A FREE budgeting note book – just pay postage.
  Again something that could be sourced from
  China and shipped out for less than £5.

- A £95 fix your finances session.

A word of warning

A customer attraction magnet is not a voucher. It's not a
percentage saving or money off, that's a voucher, a
coupon – and that's not what we're trying to do. We're
here to make money and to identify anything that
prevents us from making that money efficiently.

The goal is to give customers something tangible,
something that stacks the value, something that can act
as a demonstration of power.

Making Stuff Happen

EXERCISE #4:
Decide on your customer attraction magnet

Remember:

- This ideally should be scaled-down version of your full product or service
- It needs to be created quickly & inexpensively
- It needs to deliver results in advance for the customer and act as a demonstration of power for what you do

What is your customer attraction magnet offer?

What is the price point?

CHAPTER 6

The Profit Pumping Effect Of The Pre-Frame

The Three Things You Must Do When A Contact First Makes Contact To Quickly And Easily Get A Yes ...

With a list of proven buyers now at your fingertips, your next objective is to make sure that you and your business are seen and viewed exactly as you want to be seen by those people that have given you money. This is something you have to do as you warm them up to spending on your core offers and bigger ticket items.

We call this 'creating a frame' or 'pre-framing'.

It's the art of trying to ensure that buying more from you is the most logical and viable decision that any customer could be making.

So, why do we need to do it?

Well, ultimately, what you want to do is make any "selling" as easy as possible. I hate sleazy sales pitches as much as the next guy and this is the best way to do it.

Here's what a good pre-frame will allow you do to:

- Control your customer's experience, so you can steer it, own it and control what they know about you.

- Make sure that your prospects are making decisions and choices on YOUR terms, NOT theirs.

- Allow YOU to set the buying criteria, so the customer will logically want to choose you over your competitors.

All this control may seem a little over the top, but if left to their own devices, most people will wander around aimlessly and not be equipped to make a well-educated decision. It's exactly why it's your duty to help them. If you don't, then human nature will kick in and they won't decide.

Procrastinating on decisions is what people do. You need to make sure that you frame the entire buying experience with you, so that when it comes to the decision – choosing you is the most logical one.

Warming Up Your Customers Before The Big Show

Think of the pre-frame as the warm up act before the big show. This warm up act needs to be good, but if you're sat there thinking – *yeah but not as good as the main gig right?!*

Well YEAH actually.

FACT: Prince used to be the warm up act for the Rolling Stones.

Prince! Arguably by some, way better than the Stones. So why did the Rolling Stones have Prince as their warm up act?

Because Prince could work the crowd up into a raving frenzy.

Every heard of a shit Prince gig?

Nope, thought not - he was phenomenal, and this worked in the Stones favour. Why? Because when they hit the stage, it didn't matter what state they were in. Wrecked, high as a kite, off their face – it made no difference. The crowd was already having a great time. They were ready. They were excited. No matter the performance from the Stones, it would be perceived as awesome regardless.

Spot The Six-Figure Difference

Now I (Charlie) speak all over the world, delivering a lot of what you're reading about today on an international platform. Whenever left to an event organiser to introduce me onto the stage – they cock it up. And I've had some corkers. Compare the two intros below:

"Welcome on stage, Charlie Hutton."

OR

"It's my honour to welcome on stage our next speaker Charlie Hutton. Charlie is a bestselling author, consultant and entrepreneur and has written extensively about the subjects of marketing and business-building. In his books, workshops and seminars he teaches business owners how to dramatically increase leads, prospects and sales while minimizing their marketing expenses.

He's been referred to as a 'Direct Response Aficionado On Steroids,' and as part of his consulting activity Charlie's clients range from large national corporates, like Center Parcs, Microsoft and Tefal to TV and radio celebrities, as well as many small but mighty entrepreneurial businesses.

Be prepared for a hurricane of ideas, step by step strategy and some frantic note taking. Please put your hands together for Charlie Hutton..."

Which would have you sat up in your seat? Which do you think has the biggest impact? Which one do you think is responsible for a six-figure payday?

Note how in the second example the audience is pre-framed as to who I am, what they could expect, and why it's going to be awesome. By the time I get on stage, they're super excited, motivated, on the edge of their seats and clapping.

Contrast that to the first example, which invokes nothing but a tumble weed silence. It makes all the difference. It's the same when it comes to you and your business. A pre-framing experience for most should come in the form of a series of strategic pieces of follow up communications.

The Perfect Pre-Frame Part #1: Indoctrination

You need to be perceived as awesome no matter what. Making that happen comes down to three core elements that need to be established in your new leads and prospects:

- Credibility
- Engagement
- Likeability

Here's a sample framework to chain these things together via email over those first vital seven days in order to indoctrinate potential customers:

- Email 1 – Welcome & Credibility
- Email 2 – Credibility / Likability Content Story #1
- Email 3 – Credibility / Likability Content Story #2
- Email 4 – Engagement Statement / Question
- Email 5 – Engagement Follow-up Question
- Email 6 – Engagement with **Homework**
- Email 7 – Content with Question (and offer)

The Importance of Setting Homework

This is a key part of the engagement process because you want people to invest their time in you, and nothing does that better than setting them homework.

When we talk homework, we're not assigning a 5000-word dissertation on the Human Rights Act. It's a small task. A good tip is to directly ask the customer to print off the email and work through three or four questions. Set homework that relates to something they should be doing or know, to bring them closer towards their end goal.

For example, if you were in the fitness industry, homework might be based around calculating body mass index. If you're a tax accountant it might be working out some key profitability numbers.

By setting homework, you're getting people to commit time to you and to your business. An investment of time that's going to pay dividends by initially helping them solve a small problem.

That said, the real pay-off comes when they're making a choice between you or your competitors. Who do you think they're most likely to work with?

Company A: Someone they've just met for a 60 minute meeting

Company B: Who they've dedicated time to by completing homework, spent time with engaging, and have also met for a 60 minute meeting.

Homework **gets them actively thinking about YOU** and how you can help solve their problems. PLUS it positions you as the instigator in solving these problems.

Once a new lead has been indoctrinated either one of two things will have happen. One, they purchase or request a meeting with you. Or two, they're still not quite ready to buy. If that's the case that's totally cool, because you then push them into the next step of the pre-framing process.

The Perfect Pre-Frame Part #2: Incubation

With leads indoctrinated it's important to continue the framing exercise by deepening the nurturing process.

It allows you to capitalise on that time while your potential customers are thinking it over. Something to plug the gap and keep you front of mind, in-between the time you and your business are found and the actual sale happens – which let's face it could be anywhere between three hours to three years, depending on what you sell and who the customer is.

The Annuitas Group tell us that if you get this bit right, nurtured leads make 47 percent larger purchases than non-nurtured leads. In other words, if you have a system in place to keep in the forefront of people's minds while they're "thinking about it" you can **add nearly 50 percent to your bottom line**.

Unlike the indoctrination phase, incubation is like a dripping tap, not a fire hose. Incubation is done best with a regular weekly email.

How To Create Your Own Weekly Incubation Email:

1. Pick a day of the week. This can be any day – don't believe the hype that certain days are better than others.

2. Brand it. The brand name for your weekly email will be the subject line. It has to be something that people will begin to recognise. It's nice to tie the day of the week into step (1) here too if possible. Here are some examples:

- Sunday Success Stimulus (Yep that's ours!)
- Motivation Monday
- Tuesday's Top Tip
- Weight Drop Wednesdays
- Financial Friday's Flyer

3. Deliver engagement content with ZERO selling (yes really). Let's be clear, this is not a newsletter. It's focused on THEM not you. It's a peak behind the curtain of your business. Think an editorial piece, just like you might read in a magazine.

Here are some things to use:

- 'How to' and 'listicle' articles
- Stories from your personal life
- Photos and insights
- Quick tips
- Controversial opinions and confessions

You can think of it like a weekly local newspaper that gets dropped through the door, like clockwork, each and every week, keeping you on top of your customer's mind.

4. Send it on the same day EVERY week. This is the vital part of the process, it creates continuity and anticipation. The actual day makes no difference, it just needs to be consistent.

Here's an example of the Sunday Success Stimulus – which goes out each and every Sunday, like clock work:

"Re-Brand Yourself Into Having No Competition"

From the desk of Charlie Hutton

Sunday, May 8, 2016

Dear Ericka,

You know what, I get it...

.. You've offer a great product or service, you 're in a great market and there's lots of money to be made.

... BUT there's a ton of demand and lots of competition : (

So, Next step?

Well... Re-brand yourself so that you no longer have any real competition.

Call yourself and your business something that no one else owns.

For example, there are tons of accountants and bookkeepers out there, so you wouldn't want to call yourself by the same title as everyone else.

Instead, become a Tax Minimising expert, or a Expense Reduction consultant. Or even create your own accounting niche, such as Guerrilla Accounting or Duct Tape Accounting!

You get the picture...

Think of it this way - You want to be #1 at something new, versus #100 at something old.

Until next time,

Charlie "The Lead Gen Rockstar" Hutton

Charlie Hutton
"Online Lead Gen' Rockstar"
charlie@charliehutton.co.uk
office: 0121 288 4977

NOTE: It's during this incubation phase that you'll also want to push people through other seasonal, or promotional, campaigns that nudge them towards taking action.

Automating for ZERO Human Error, Minimum Effort, And Maximum Predictability!

Although both an indoctrination and incubation phase can be done manually, it's impossible to scale without automation. Automating this essential nurture process stops leads slipping through the cracks.

Automation Step #1: Choose your automation tool

All you need is a simple email auto responder. You have lots of choice here, depending on your budget.

Our top recommendation at the time of press, and if you're just getting started, is Active Campaign. Cost ranges from £9 to £49 per month. It's a great starter automation tool because you can trigger things based on people's actions, with zero input from you.

Other options include MailChimp, cost ranges from free to £199 per month, and GetResponse cost ranges from £10 to £110 per month.

We use Infusionsoft. This starts at around £150, so it's not cheap, but it's functionality for marketing automation is where you want to be. If you can afford a tool like this, it's a no brainer!

Automation Step #2: Build out your campaign

Whichever platform you choose, creating the campaign is usually simple; just a drag and drop process:

- Drag out an email
- Edit the contents
- Set a time delay until next email

Automation Step #3: Work out your timings

When it comes to the delay between emails in the sequence it's good to hit them every day for the first seven days when indoctrinating. In markets where communication needs to be a little less frequent (which is very few, by the way). A good fall back to use is a Fibonacci sequence, or what is sometimes called the "Golden Ratio".

Don't worry. It's not complicated. It's just a series of numbers where the next number is found by adding up the two numbers before it. Fibonacci sequences are found in patterns everywhere in nature, from flower petals to animal flight paths!

Now when applied to an indoctrination sequence it might look like this:

- Email 1 (no delay)
- Email 2 (wait a day)

- Email 3 (wait a day)
- Email 4 (wait two days)
- Email 5 (wait three days)
- Email 6 (wait five days)
- Email 7 (wait eight days)

Making Stuff Happen

EXERCISE #5:
Your Indoctrination Sequence.

Ok. So this is not a 15-minute job, but once these bad boys are created, the content will last you an age.

1. Write the topics for your seven-day indoctrination sequence.
2. Load up your indoctrination campaign into your chosen automated email software mail.
3. Write your first four weekly incubation emails.

Indoctrination Email Topics:

What day of the week will you send your weekly incubation email?

What is the brand name for your weekly incubation email?

CHAPTER 7

The Covert Commitment Stack For Sure Fire Sales

A Simple, Little Known, Psychological Secret That Makes A Customer TWICE As Likely To Buy From You...

S o, after attracting a quality customer, framing everything to perfection, next comes The Covert Commitment Stacker. This is the part of the process where we'll start to see the fruits of all the hard work so far.

The Covert Commitment Stack uses simple psychological triggers of influence; foundations that have been built on from Robert Cialdini and his book "Influence". If you've not read it, once you're done here go to amazon and snag yourself a copy – you won't be disappointed.

Robert Cialdini talks about the six psychological triggers of influence as being:

- Reciprocation
- Social Proof
- Commitment and Consistency
- Liking
- Authority
- Scarcity

You'll notice a couple have already been used in the pre-frame process, and in the Commitment Stack you'll build on this to get maximum impact.

The goal here is to make sure that when someone's coming in to a meeting with you, they are coming in armed with the best mindset possible in order to buy from you. The commitment stack comes into the sales process after any framing, and before any proper sales conversation. Usually in a B2B environment when an appointment is requested.

When To Use For Maximum Impact

Commitment stacking works best when a potential customer is raising their hand for the first time to try to speak to you. It comes after the frame, and before any proper sales conversation.

Right about here:

| First contact | Nurture & engage | Sales conversation | Sale |

The BIG Problem

So you've gone to all this effort to attract these prospects; turning them to buyers, indoctrinating them, and that's when most tend to sit back, take five minutes and say:

"Hot diggity, I am good! Someone wants to buy my stuff! I am a Marketing Genius!"

You give yourself a big pat on the back. You can't wait to have a meeting with this piping hot prospect. You think you've done great, you ARE great, and you think that this person must also think the same. And therefore, the money is already in the bank.

... and that's the worst, WORST, WORRRRRST thing you can do. Now is the time you really need to work and do what 99 percent of your competitors will not be doing.

Because the reality of life is even at this stage, so close to the goal, you are still probably in a situation where you'll be quoting against competitors.

Why?

Well because people, and most importantly business people, do their due diligence. Chances are they will still go out to three, maybe even five, other providers of whatever it is that you do, to get some quotes. Trouble is you can quickly end up in a bidding war, or worse yet a race to the bottom on price.

This sound familiar:

"Joe Blogs is going to do it for so £X cheaper than you – can you match it?"

And before you know it, you're screwed.

You MUST INTERRUPT his process.

Like everything else you've uncovered today, you need to control this experience by making sure that when someone wants to have that conversation or meeting with you, you do something which is completely counter intuitive to most people.

You make them apply to speak to you.

Yeah, that's right. You put them through an application process to speak to you. Sounds crazy right? But you must at all costs, take control back of the experience, in a manner that's along the lines of:

"Hey, it's awesome that you want to have a conversation with us about how we might be able to help. We are ever

so slightly different to everyone else. If you want to have a chat, we've got a short application form that you will need to fill out and complete in order for us to have a conversation with you."

Now, there's a couple of psychological things at play here, the biggest being that this process gets them to create another micro commitment. This is where the stacking principle comes in because they've already committed time during the indoctrination phase by engaging with the homework, so once an application form is complete the level of commitment is stacked and compounded.

Application Process Step #1: The Form

The application form has three key goals:

1. Collect FULL contact details: The reason why will become very clear in the next chapter (ohhh suspense!)

Full really means full:

- Name
- Mobile
- E-mail address
- Website
- Physical address
- Phone number

2. Start To Establish the Gap: This is the gap between where they are now and where they want to be. You see a good application form will trying to find and extract the pain points that this prospect has, and what the real reason behind that pain is. Here are some great questions are:

- Where are you now?
- Where would you like to be?
- Why have you decided to look for help now?
- What have you tried already and hasn't worked and why?
- Where would you like to be 12 months down the line for this to be a success?

If possible, get the customer to put actual physical numbers around this so they can start seeing the pain in the cold hard light of day stuff. The physical gap between where they are now and where they want to be. The psychology behind this is starting to get them to really open up, to the point where they are, or aren't, and why they need to fix this problem now.

Information is vital when it comes to actually selling them on a solution, as you can sell to their exact specific problems – rather than with features and benefits.

3. Get Them to Sell YOU: Ask them to tell you why they would be a great customer for YOU and why YOU should take them on board as a client!

I know that sounds kind of crazy. It's completely counter intuitive to what you have probably heard before – but there is a science behind it. It's often referred to as Pendulum selling.

You see, the majority of businesses will go out there and they will sell themselves silly on why they are a good business for a client to deal with.

Your goal now is to completely turn the tables and say:

"Hey, you know what? Why don't you tell me why you think you are a good client?"

Ballsy I know. You might even be thinking there ain't a chance in hell someone will fill that out – but you're wrong!

People will and they do.

They will sit and write you a mini essay on how great they are to work with. And of course, as people, when they start selling themselves on why they are a good person for you to deal with, they are selling themselves to themselves on why they should be doing business with you. Essentially they themselves are reinforcing their commitment and doing your selling for you.

The best bit is this takes away all the pain and all the headaches of having to do any 'sales pitch' when you meet. You are no longer pitching; they are selling themselves on why they should be working with you.

Application Process Step #2: The Homework

Yes. I know it's like ground hog day. But as part of this application process it is vital to set the customer more homework. Homework that needs to be completed by them before you meet. It's all about constant reinforcement.

Homework at this application stage could come in the form of getting them to:

- Watch a video online
- Complete an assignment or an audit
- Collect together some information

Ideally it needs to revolve around a small task that needs to be completed before you next meet – assuming of course the application is successful! ;-)

Remember, if someone is going to sit through additional training online via our video, or if they're going to complete an audit, or if someone's going to spend half an hour, 20 minutes, or even just 10 minutes doing an exercise, they're infinitely more engaged with you as a business.

They are closer to you than they will ever be to any of your competitors; you're forging deeper-rooted psychological bonds.

Application Process Step #3: Choose The Best, Refer The Rest

With an application form complete, the next step is simple – decide if you think you want them as customer! Do you think they'll be a good fit for you and how you help people?

This allows you to handpick customers and work with only those that you want to work with.

Good Applicant Criteria:

1) Lots Of Information Given: If someone fills out the forms and puts lots of detail down then they are probably a lot warmer of a prospect than someone who gives an answer of a few words.

The more information that's on the form the more pain they are in, suggesting that they are more likely to buy. This is as good as a buying signal gets!

2) They Tell You They're Good: How good a job did they do on selling themselves as a customer?

3) Level of Urgency: A great question to ask is:

How serious are you about solving [inert problem] on a scale of 1-10?

People that answer 6 or above are probably the ones that are most likely to spend.

If you think they'll be a good fit (and someone you can help) that's great –follow up and get the meeting booked.

Referring The Rest

It goes without saying, not everyone will be a good fit and that's OK. Why not simply refer them to someone?

Just because they're not a fit for you doesn't necessarily mean that they're not an ideal customer for someone else. In fact, chances are for someone else, they could be a Grade A, triple platinum, best ever client material.

Here's how that conversation goes:

"Hey, John thanks for the application. Unfortunately I don't think we're going to be able to help you. This isn't really a good fit for us, but we've got a great guy over here called, Dave. Dave deals in this sort of thing all day long. We think he will be an awesome for you. We've passed your details on so expect Dave to give you a call in the next couple of days."

Far from ruining this relationship, you've done the exact opposite. You've become a trusted advisor by recommending that they go and speak to someone else, someone better suited to help them with their specific problems.

On top of this, whoever you've just referred them to will think you're a rock star for passing on a red hot lead.

I know what you're thinking:

"There's not a cat in hell's chance that this is going to work in my business. It's going to put people off. No one is going to complete this form. No one is going to go through all of this rigmarole."

Let's prove you wrong by showing some of the responses we've seen clients get from people after they've just got the "you've been accepted for a meeting notification…"

Here are a couple of 'normal' responses that we've seen:

Real Response Example #1

"Oh Wow!!! I'm so thrilled – thank you! I promise to do all of the homework and everything you need from me ASAP. I have meetings until 6pm today, but as soon as I can I'll get cracking on this."

Real Response Example #2

Thank you for this, I'm really pleased, this will help the company a lot. Have a nice day!

…. And here is a personal favourite that's now referred to as the "screaming orgasm." If you hadn't guessed, it's how the book got its title of the "Orgasm Effect":

Real Response Example #3

OMG!!!! I CAN'T BELIEVE I'VE BEEN CHOSEN!! I'M OVER THE MOON!

I'm ecstatic! I really don't know how much to say thank you – there just aren't any words to describe how I'm feeling right now – ELATED is an understatement. Gosh – and thanks again – WOW!

How powerful is that?

When was the last time you got an e-mail like that from one of your customers, let alone from a new lead and a new prospect, just because they were having the opportunity to have a conversation with you?

YES the process is definitely counter intuitive to traditional marketing.

YES you're making people jump through a lot of hoops.

YES you do lose people along the way.

BUT that's what makes this so effective at putting you on the path to sure-fire sales after committing so much. It's the culmination of everything that's happened over the last six chapters. Ask yourself this;

Do you think it might be easier to convert one of these prospects over one that's just picked up the phone for a chat?

Good – thought so. So now let's quickly just summarize The Covert Commitment Stack:

- Step 1- Everyone applies to meet with you.
- Step 2 – Set them homework.
- Step 3 – Choose the best, refer the rest.

Now over to you to make this happen for your business.

Making Stuff Happen

EXERCISE #6:
Crafting Your Application Form

List the 3-5 questions that you'll ask on your application form:

What homework will you set?

CHAPTER 8

The Secret To Showing Up Like No One Else

The "Secret Sauce" To Out Marketing Your Competitors And Making More Money...

O k so if you've done everything up to this point, you've done a good job at attracting people that spend money, you've demonstrated you know what you're talking about, and, after the Covert Commitment Stack, the people who are coming to meet you should now be orgasmically excited about what's happening.

The next step is vital, and by using one simple tactic you'll ensure:

- You never compete apples for apples.
- You never haggle on price.

- You never have to "sell" again.

It's done by showing up like no one else– something often referred to as Shock N Awe!

CASE STUDY: The Power Of Shock N Awe In A Price Sensitive Market

We moved house recently, part of which meant we signed up for a new mortgage provider. Now when it comes to getting a mortgage, the market couldn't be more cut throat. Just try Googling "Mortgage Provider" and you're bombarded with one-click instant price comparison websites. Not a good place to be selling.

Anyway, we signed up for a deal online with a UK provider Nationwide. There was nothing special about the sales process BUT the after sales process was some of the best I've ever seen.

You see, the day we moved into our new property by 2pm, we were stressed, we were sweating, we were tired - the usual moving day fun and games. And that's when there was a knock at the door.

It was a UPS guy with a HUGE box addressed to us both – which left us very puzzled as to who the hell

---

had our address as we'd only been in the property no more than three hours!

It was from the new mortgage lender. They'd sent a big box of stuff to say, "Welcome to your new home."

Talk about Shock N Awe – we were amazed. They'd filled this thing to the brim with things like magazines, vouchers, breakfast cereals, toilet tissues, tea bags, coffee, mugs and much more.

It was our very own house moving supply kit!

An absolute fantastic example of showing up like no one else. A mortgage is a very transactional sale – the problem being that when it comes to renewal you have no bond or allegiance to your provider. By doing this, the provider have not only delivered an epic amount of good will, virtually guaranteed that we will renew with them and of course we told everyone we know about it (even going so far as to write about it in this book), PLUS we've opened a new savings account with them since.

This box probably cost them all of £30 to put together, but even if it cost £300 it was a great investment. They know how much we're worth to them over their lifetime.

As part of the moving process we also dealt with removals guys, solicitors and even storage companies – how many of them do you think sent us anything?

Not one – not even a card!

To get the maximum effect with your customers and prospects your Shock N Awe box must adhere to five golden rules:

Rule #1: It must rattle.

Rule #2: It must include something yum to TASTE, because let's face it, everyone loves a treat.

Rule #3: It must use different types of paper that feel different to TOUCH.

Rule #4: It must include some audio/visual element that can be HEARD or SEEN.

Rule #5: It must come in a box for maximum impact. It makes people feel like it's Christmas, and who doesn't love opening a big surprise on Christmas day?

Ultimately, when the box gets opened, the goal is for a ton of things to drop out and fall all over the table so they can almost sift and explore through everything. You want to make this a fun adventure for the person receiving, something they can explore and uncover.

Your goal here is to create a *"WTF Have you seen this thing it's awesome"* response from your prospect.

The 8 Essential Elements To Surprise & Delight

- A cover letter
- A book
- An offer
- A transformation blueprint
- Credibility pieces
- Audio CD or DVD Video
- Chocolate!

Surprise & Delight Element #1: Cover Letter.

Your cover letter should be no more than two sides of A4 and outline the following:

1. Explain WHY you're sending the box.
2. Explain WHY they made a good decision
3. Explain WHAT will happen next.
4. Explain WHAT is in the box.
5. Explain WHEN they need to take action.

Surprise & Delight Element #2: A Book

When it comes to a book there's a couple of things you can do.

One - If you've got your own book, then you should include a signed copy – it's the greatest business card ever. It does awesome things for your status and your positioning.

Two - If you don't have your own book, go have a look around Amazon and find a book on the marketplace that gives a high level overview of what you do.
These books will probably cost you around £5 a pop, no more than £10, a miniscule investment considering the impact it will add.

Books are a great way to add weight to the box, more credibility (even implied credibility if it's not your book), and it engages people. It's that sort of thing that will linger around on a desk, or around at home, reminding them of who you are and what you do.

Surprise & Delight Element #3: A Special Offer

By the time someone is at the stage of getting a Shock N Awe box, they're probably the hottest prospect under the sun – that's why it's vital that you make them an offer at this stage to take the relationship further.

Ideally you should offer something that will compliment and not contradict the service that you'll present when you meet.

Surprise & Delight Element #4: A Transformation Blueprint

Remember your Results in Advanced Timeline from Chapter 3? Well you want to include a copy in your box. It's best if you give your timeline to a graphic designer to make it look like a road map to success.

Of course your "braded" benefit loaded transformation headline should be front and centre where possible also try to use benefit-loaded phrases to describe the milestones that you'll help them overcome.

Your transformation blueprint will do two things:

1) Give the customer a simple, easy to follow diagram of exactly how you will help them solve their problem.

2) Differentiate you from everyone else that is selling the same old boring services.

Surprise & Delight Element #5: Credibility Pieces

You need no more than two of these. It could even be a selection of the following:

- Copies of magazine or newspaper articles that have been written by or about you.
- Press clippings about successes.
- Client transformation case studies.
- Copies of blog posts or other online hero content you've published.

The goal here is to give proof that you're in the public eye, that you're doing the thing that you're promising you can do, that you do it regularly, and that you do it well.

Don't worry; if you're starting out and haven't got any of this yet just create some yourself. Write a simple article and get a graphic designer to mock it up so it looks like it's been in a magazine. Make sure it's relevant to what you're taking to the customer about, that it puts you in a good light and delivers goodwill.

Surprise & Delight Element #6: Audio CD or DVD Video

The audio or visual element can be as simple as taking one of the following items and getting them put on a CD or DVD:

- A recording of a webinar or podcast.
- An MP3 of a talk you've done on stage.

- A business video you've had done for your website.

Now, if you've not got anything pre-recorded, the good news is that you can pretty much create an audio from scratch in about 60 minutes. Here's what you do:

Step #1: Grab your smart phone.
Step #2: Take your results in advanced time.
Step #3: Talk through the process.

Make sure you also include:

- An explanation at the start of exactly what it is you're about to talk about.
- The reason why you're doing this (HINT: to help people get from A to B).
- Your story. Let the listener know what your background is, where you've come from, what you've done, and how you've come to this point.

The finished article doesn't need to be long – 20 to 30 minutes will more than suffice.

Another shortcut is to get a friend or colleague to do a quick interview with you and ask you some questions. Record the interview – job done.

Surprise & Delight Element #6: Testimonials

Some undeniable proof of your awesomeness. Where possible try to have a range of these that you can use. If possible, showcase testimonials that are relative to the customer – use people, business types, locations, and business sizes that are similar. This similarity will help build appeal. If you have a testimonial from someone or some business that's aspirational to your customer - get that in there too.

The goal here is to whittle down any barriers with a bunch of amazing testimonials.

You can never have enough social proof, so the more testimonials the better. If that means it spans over three to four books then so be it. You want people to think:

"Man, these guys have helped a ton of people and they've all got awesome results – I'd be stupid not to choose them."

IMPORTANT – Make sure you re-read Chapter 4 on how to capture transformational testimonials, there's a reason we told you this. It's so you could apply it here.

Surprise & Delight Element #7: Chocolate

Anything that is edible will work here, to tie in the sense of taste, and trigger the psychological reaction of trust that comes with eating and rapport that's build by "breaking bread" with a stranger.

If the chocolate doesn't fit with your business, (e.g. A personal trainer) you can use coffee or other consumable alternative.

Surprise & Delight Element BONUS Element: Rules for Business

Here's an optional extra for you, we call it "My Rules."

It's a simple double-sided postcard that explains your rules for business, who your ideal client is, who you work best with and, most importantly, what you like and don't like.

This is another one of those counter intuitive things. But when implemented it gives you the power to start this new relationship on your terms. From the outset you're laying out the ground rules of what they should expect from you and how they can expect the relationship to evolve.

Plus it helps if you have any come back at later stages, because you outline the brief terms of service upfront, right at the outset.

Below is an example of one of our original rule cards. Note how it clearly sets the expectations around dress code and work hours, without being too over the top. It also throws some humour in there as the last point to soften the statements previous.

I love doing what I do and in order to make sure that continues I have a set of non negotiable rules when taking on clients:

RULE 1: <u>FUN</u>

A wise man once told me "don't take life too seriously – you'll never get out alive!" Life is short, so lets enjoy it.

RULE 2: <u>NO TIES EVER</u>

Can't stand them, I didn't wear one to my wedding and wearing one is something that I will not do for money :)

RULE 3: <u>FAMILY</u>

My Family comes first. This works both ways, so if there's a time where we must choose between the two, I say lets pick family.

RULE 4: <u>VALUE OF SERVICES GIVEN</u>

If you want cheap, a quick fix or a "magic bullet" I'm not for you. However if you want ultimate value, based on my years of experience, education and expertise then lets talk.

RULE 5: <u>TASTE IN MUSIC</u>

My liking country music is not a crime! I will however accept gentle mocking and the occasional "yee-ha."

The True Cost of Shock N Awe

Totalled up, most Shock N Awe boxes come in at around £10 for everything – contents and postage.

If you push the boat out and include premium packing, printing and top notch chocolate, you'll still be under £25. I'm sure for most of you this is a drop in the water compared to the revenue generated from signing up a new client.

That's why it's an INVESTMENT not a cost.

Let me ask you this:

How many times would you spend £25 if you could turn it into £250, £2500 or maybe even £25,000 three days down the line?

It's not essential but you might also consider the use of a courier or guaranteed delivery. In the grand scheme of things it's not that expensive and will give you peace of mind that it's got to the right person.

Ideally your Shock N Awe box should land three to five days before you meet. Leaving enough time for the customer to go through the contents, but not too long that the excitement from rummaging around and exploring the contents had been lost.

Remember these people have gone through your indoctrination process, they've applied to meet with you and they've jumped through a lot of hoops. These are highly qualified prospects that deserve to be treated;

you're not sending these out to the great-unwashed masses!

Ask yourself these quick questions:

- Is anyone else in your market doing this?
- Is anyone else going to be showing up like this before a meeting?
- Is anyone else giving this customer this experience?

Experience would suggest the answer is No, No and No.

Make sure you capitalise, and more importantly show up like no one else.

CASE STUDY: The £24,000 Picnic Hamper

A private Mastermind client, Osmond Maguire from Wizard Technical Designs Ltd (www.wtdesigns.co.uk) sent out a Shock N Awe box to a client after a sales meeting. He was competing with three other much bigger more established firms, so showing up like no one else was a must.

He sent the overflowing hamper the day after the meeting:

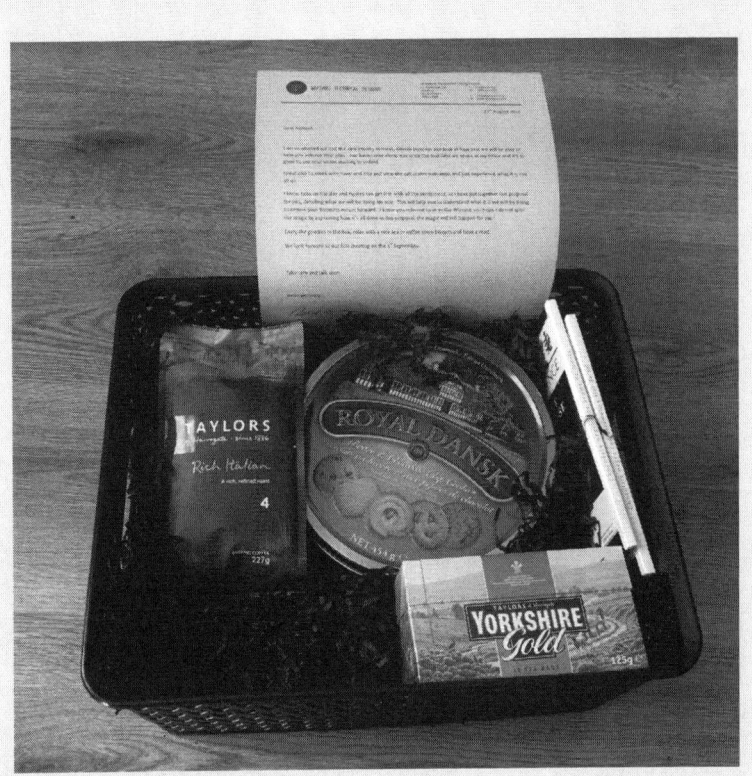

He used recorded delivery to make sure that the box got there at 1PM. At 1.30PM he got a phone call thanking him for the hamper, all the goodies inside, plus they signed him up there and then for a contract worth £24,000. They didn't even bother seeing the other three service providers to get quotes or estimates.

Making Stuff Happen

EXERCISE #7:
Putting together your Shock N Awe Box

Now it's time to decide on the contents of your box:

CHAPTER 9

Eight Life Lessons That Will Save You From Losing Your Shirt

The Things We Wish Someone Had Told Us In The Beginning...

Lesson #1: Bigger Profits From Smaller Lists

Lots of people will tell you it's all about the size of your list. The bigger your email list, list of contacts or whatever, the bigger the opportunity that's waiting to be seized.

We bought into this hook, line and sinker. Spent a ton of money on building up a BIG email list when we first started out, money we didn't have to waste.

Trouble was the herd of people we'd gathered weren't ever going to buy a thing. Sitting back and working out the numbers it became clear that the ROI was through the floor.

We went through and exercised and culled all the people that hadn't clicked or opened an email from us in 90 days. Net result was we lost nearly 80 percent of our contacts in one fell swoop.

The impact on sales?

Zero. The buyers were, and still are, in the engaged 20 percent.

So let's be clear, size is not important; it's about how engaged people are with you and what you're offering. The more engaged they are, the more likely they'll respond. The more they respond, the more they'll buy. The more they buy, the better your return on investment.

That said, lead generation is still a HUGE part of the monthly activity – as fresh new prospects are the life-blood of any business. But we are now much more targeted in what we are looking for (ideal clients only please). PLUS we are willing to spend much, much more to get that ideal person into our lists.

Each and every month we do a regular cull on the list! Yep, we take the time to permanently cull people from our list based on 90-day engagement. We send them one last email, called the 'last chance saloon,' and if they don't respond we let them go.

This monthly cull is good practice. And it helps us too. We know our 'proper' number, and that means we can calculate our performance, response targets etc.

Lesson #2: More is More

The other mistake that cost us dearly was the classic trap of less is more. We didn't want to 'bombard' people with offers or information to get responses. We thought the awesomeness of what we do would shine through and people would naturally feel like getting in touch.

We were wrong. Less is less. Less communication equals less response. And as a result of this 'less is more' communication mistake in the early years, we let lots of potential buyers slip through our fingers.

More communication equals more response. More response equals more sales.

ALWAYS.

Sometimes that has meant sending people up to five emails a day – yes five!! If it's important, if it's relevant, and if it will help them, send as many as it takes.

Lesson #3: Mass Is Trash

Once we got over the less is more trap, the next mistake we made was pretty hefty.

We'd take our engaged list and communicate the same message, at the same time, to everyone on our list.

This was a mistake.

We were making the assumption that all customers, prospects and leads were *ready* to receive that message at the same time. They were not. Somebody that had already been in our world for a year is not in the same place as a new contact!

We needed to get smarter. We needed to pick our moment. Timing separates the professional from the amateur.

We needed to give people a bespoke experience to increase response. We spent hours mapping and creating bespoke driven customer journeys for each type of lead:

Things to look for when creating customer journeys include:

- Where did this person enter your world?
- What valuable content can you give them related to this first entry path?
- What does this mean they are MOST likely to be interested in from your offered products and services?
- What's the right way to offer it e.g. Webinar, Video, Direct Mail, Face to Face?
- If there is no response from this campaign, what is the next most appropriate offer to send them?

Then it's just rinse and repeat for the next offer.

Lesson #4: Spend!

You have to be willing to spend on the tools you need for the job.

For us, we realised it was all about customer focused journeys and response.

Manually doing this stuff was possible. Although we were making it work, our unwillingness to spend the money on tools and systems was crippling us. To make a change was a big monthly investment. We were nervous. We didn't spend the money.

Once we finally bit the bullet and made the investment in our automation stack, it transformed everything – more time, more response, more money.

This 'lesson' also applies to your marketing budget too.

You must be willing to spend more on traffic. Whether than be Facebook, LinkedIn, Direct Mail, whatever works for your business.

If only we had £10 for every time we saw someone spend a load of money and time creating campaigns, simply to go at it with a tiny advertising spend or only give it a week, deem it a failure and turn it off!

It's false economy! You must be willing to spend money on that traffic. Test audiences. Test new media. Start wide, then get narrow, then scale, scale, scale.

We reinvested every last pound we could afford back into testing and the scaling. It helped us grow at pace. Did some of our campaigns flop? Absolutely! But we learnt, we got better, we learnt from our mistakes and found out where not to focus.

We still reinvest everything we can afford. These days we are always willing to spend. You should be too.

Lesson #5: Response - Then What?

So, you get the response you are after, you make the sale - WOOOHOOO! Happy days, right?!

No. Well, obviously yes, but you need to be much more strategic. You need to really think about what you do in that immediate time, after the sale.

Take as much effort in this as you've done with your whole process up to this point. It's really just as important.

In the meantime, here are our top three pointers for post-sale follow up:

1) Deliver excellent value to this new customer as quickly as possible, so that they feel like they have made the best decision in spending with you.

2) Say thank you. Apply the same Shock N Awe principle to a 'welcome on board' pack. Put things in there that will set up the relationship for success. Have they spent a load of money with you? Think about a thank you gift, make it personal – no selling!

3) Check in. The start of any relationship is the best time to knock them dead and build a great relationship. To do this you need to know how you are doing, so stay in touch. In person or on the phone is best. Fix any niggles quickly and smoothly.

By creating a great relationship in the early phase it means that you can hit the jackpot because...

Lesson #6: Retaining Your Customers Is Free Money

Keeping a customer happy and getting repeat purchases from them is free, easy money. It is often the forgotten sister to the more glamourous initial sale but it shouldn't be. Repeating customers and getting them to spend more will always deliver a better return on your investment.

You should always be thinking about the best way to retain your customers from the moment they come on board. From that moment on, you need to be thinking what's next.

Think about what additional services or product would be a good fit for this customer, and when is the most effective time to position those? If you are looking to retain a contract, work back from the contract end date. You need to have retained that customer well before anyone else approaches them where possible.

Lesson #7: No one cares about your business

This is a really important but brutal one, so brace yourself. No one cares about your business as much as you do.

So don't sweat the small stuff - it's not as a big deal as you think. It's the big stuff that matters. You need to get to grips with really understanding what you're selling and who you're selling to.

Who are your ideal customers? What industries are they in? What's the size of their business? Where are they? What are their motivators? What are their interests? What do you have in common?

Create well thought out customer profiles and personalities and use all this to get the response you are after.

Lesson #8: Leap frogging isn't cheating

So this one is more of a 'mental' shift compared to a practical lesson, but an important one none the less.

You do not need to follow the traditional path of growth. If you can leap frog and hack your way there quicker, then do it.

For example, here is the traditional path to success for a lawyer in the UK:

- Take law degree
- Do LPC
- Do training contract
- Get first newly qualified job
- Work your way up to Associate
- Work your way up to Partner
- Maybe take a seat on a bench
- Retire

All in all, for a lawyer to get to the place of proper weight, status and making big bucks they need to make Partner. And that takes years. Lots of them. Maybe 20 of them!

You can fall into the same trap in your business if you're careful. Thinking that you need to pay your dues to get the success you deserve. Let's be clear, this is NOT TRUE.

Here's how you can leapfrog to the top in any industry:

Leap frog strategy #1: Surround yourself with good people. Yes, it's a bit woo, but this really works. Surround yourself with great people, professionally and personally. You always want to be 'the worst house on the street', always be looking upwards. Surround yourself with people doing great things. Learn from them, take it as inspiration.

Leap frog strategy #2: Get a mentor. Find someone who has done something you want to do; maybe they get great speaking gigs, or have broken into an industry you want to. Whatever it may be, find them and ask them to mentor you.

Think people won't want to mentor you? Think again. It is seriously flattering. You think they are great and want to learn from them! It doesn't need to be a big commitment. We've had valuable mentoring relationships where we meet for a couple of hours every quarter.

This mentoring means you can listen to their wisdom, avoid all the mistakes they made and leap frog to success.

Leap frog strategy #3: Masterminding. Masterminds are always phenomenal for business. Spend a lot of time researching a good mastermind group, look for the best you can afford. You will always get a good return on your investment.

You will make great connections, learn great things from others in the room and discover great partnering opportunities. You'll be able to leap frog potential road blocks, avoid mistakes and make great contacts.

CHAPTER 10

Our Technology Stack

Every little tool, website and resource to save you hours, weeks, if not months ...

T his chapter is a list of all the resources and technology tools we use in our business and were you can go to find them.

Places we buy help

You can pretty much buy anything you need for your marketing and anything else you need for your business right here – copy writing, design, video producers. You name it they've got it!

We buy a lot of help from Upwork especially. Our advice would be to put together a solid brief, and go with who you think will do the best job. Go with a freelancer who you think will do the best job, in the quickest timeframe you can afford.

- Upwork - https://www.upwork.com

- Fivver - https://uk.fiverr.com/

- Freelancer - https://www.freelancer.co.uk/

Marketing tools we use

- Marketing automation software: Infusionsoft: https://www.infusionsoft.com/

- Website and blogging platform: WordPress: https://wordpress.com/

- Campaign & Process Maps: Lucid Chart: https://www.lucidchart.com/

- Video Hosting: Wistia: https://wistia.com/

- Transcription: Rev https://www.rev.com/transcription

- Conversion tacking: conversionfly: https://conversionfly.com/

- Printing: Printed.com: https://www.printed.com/

Business tools we use daily

- Team communications: Slack: https://slack.com/

- Accounting: Xero: https://www.xero.com/uk/

- File storage & sharing: Google drive and dropbox: https://www.dropbox.com/

- Organisation and lists: Evernote: https://evernote.com/

Places for Inspiration

- Social Media Examiner: www.socialmediaexaminer.com

- Copy Blogger: http://www.copyblogger.com/

- Smart Marketing: https://smartmarketer.com/

- Digital marketer: http://www.digitalmarketer.com/

- Swipe Worthy: http://swiped.co/

BONUS CHAPTERS

CHAPTER 11

Getting A Response From Corporates

By Emma Hutchinson

Most entrepreneurs and small business owners dream of happy customer lists that include a corporate giant or two like HP, Tesco, Tefal or Cadburys. Sadly, though, most people believe that the 'Corp' is a tough nut to crack, so huge that they don't even know where to start and they question why a corporate would ever want to do business with them.

The truth is that winning a corporate customer is no harder, or easier, to win than any other customer. But I will admit to them being downright intimidating from the outside!

How do we know? Well, we've (Emma has) spent over ten years in the corporate game. So here's the inside track on how to get response from a corporate.

1. Corporate are always buying a shed-load of help
And you can be one of them.

From the outside you might think, why would they need it when the employ so many people?!

And they do employ a lot of people! In my last role my UK team was 15,000, globally getting close to 100,000. The UK Customer Service team had over 5,000 people alone. The marketing team that was my home had over 200.

But these people just aren't enough. In the marketing team we had over 30 people in communications alone. You'd think they could handle everything to do with our communications right? Well, not when we have over seven million accounts, plus above the line; including multi-million-pound TV advertising and below the line direct communications to manage for over seven million customers.

So we bought in help when we needed it and it worked a treat. We outsourced, used contractors and bought agencies.

Corporates have the funds to buy help and they do. ALWAYS. Why? It's quicker than recruiting, they want to work with experts, and they want it done yesterday.

Which leads onto the second point...

2. Corporates will pay the big bucks for a specialist

People tend to do similar things in corporates and teams are made up of generalists. And they need to be, everyone covers for everyone else.

What a corporate wants to buy is a specialist. They will pay top whack. Why? Because a specialist can help the corporate a lot. They can do something the corporate's team cannot do themselves. The specialist has the opportunity to add so much value that a corporation will keep coming back again and again.

They will pay over and above to get the BEST help around.

Find your niche and own it. Big companies can be virtual gold mines for savvy entrepreneurs. If they like your product or service, they'll eagerly expand their relationship with you. You'll be much more successful if you focus on solving a small or overlooked need that the company is facing. This enables you to slip in under the radar screen of any entrenched suppliers who own the account.

Keep in mind...

3. Sales is NOT just a numbers game with Corporates

Don't fool yourself into thinking that landing big corporate clients is just a numbers game. Traditional sales gurus tell you to just keep dialling, smiling and making those connections. That doesn't work when you're trying to crack into big companies.

Lots of planning, creative thinking, research and persistence are needed. A strong business case is essential. Corporate decision makers demand that you come prepared—with valuable ideas, insights and information that can help them improve their own business, reduce expenses or increase revenue.

And you need to...

4. Pay the Corporate price of admission

Corporate decision makers are swamped. Seriously, we spend all day in meetings. They have way too much work to do and not nearly enough time to get it all done. They protect their time at all costs; it's their most precious resource. If you want a spot on their already overcrowded calendar, you have to earn it.

What's the price of admission? Research the company, industry and marketplace. Gain knowledge of their business issues, challenges, goals and objectives. Acquire expertise on their processes, methodologies or critical success factors. Busy decision makers don't want to take time to update you about their business. Nor do they want to learn about your offer unless they know, from the outset, that you bring value.

This mantra is a great one where thinking about corporate decision makers is concerned – "Be Bright. Be bold. Be brief. Be gone." - David Currier

Homework is key, you've got to...

5. Find the Right Person within the Corporate

A random spamming of email addresses is not the right way to go about this, because not everyone in a corporate knows each other. We're based in huge teams, in different offices, in different countries, on different continents. We don't all get together for lunch. And it's super annoying when people, especially cold contacts who email me to ask me to introduce the 'Customer Service Director'... obviously the email goes in the bin.

The right way is to research who does what. LinkedIn is your friend here. Break people down into subsets. Rather than being immobilized by the magnitude of selling to, Boots for example, you might pursue a relationship with the marketing department of the No7 brand team. This enables you to find out the names of potential decision makers, and do your due diligence without being overwhelmed.

You've also got to adapt and...

6. Speak the Corporate Language

This is so obvious between Charlie and I every single time we work together. I'm from the corporate world. He's an entrepreneur through-and-through. I say 'customer acquisition and retention'. And he says 'winning and holding onto customers'. It really means the same thing BUT if you want to win the corporate big fish you have to adapt your language.

And like selling to anyone... it's not about you, it's about them. Make it all about you and it's going to lead to an objection. Instead, talk about the results your company provides. For example, decision makers want to hear you can: speed up time on the revenue of new product launches, increase sales to new market segments, reduce supply chain costs etc. etc.

That's the language the corporate speaks. To capture their attention, you need to speak it, too. All in corporate language, but all about them and their needs.

Corporates are pretty awesome at planning so...

7. Understand WHEN Corporates buy

There is always money somewhere in a corporate. Never believe otherwise. But there are definitely easier times to access that money.

Most corporates operate budget allocation on a yearly cycle, and this usually runs on the calendar year, not at the end of the financial year. Why? Because at tax year end the account team are stacked doing the reporting, so it's easier on resource planning to do it on the calendar year to keep the bean counters busy ☺.

So ideally, to get on the budget you need to be having the conversations before year end.

A point worth remembering is that a corporate plan is never set in stone, too much changes for that, both internal and externally. Personally I see them more as guidance. For example, if we had to pull in more customers, and we needed to run a campaign quickly, and needed a great new supplier, I'd change up the allocation.

But we did have to play by the buying help rules. So you must...

8. Understand HOW Corporates Buy

How all Corporates buy is systemized and follows some sort of rules. There is no messing about outside the rules, we all play by them.

The buying system is usually a three tiered

- Tier 1 – Small spend
- Tier 2 – Middle spend
- Tier 3 – Mega spend

I'm pretty sure they had a much more corporate title than this, so sorry purchasing department if you are reading!

Tier 1 is the easiest entry point and it also gives you the opportunity to build direct relationships quickly. Then you can build up if you wish to.

And let's be clear, small spend to a corporate is not small to mere mortals; it always, always, always revolves around a magic number. In my team our magic number was £50,000... hardly small.

Under £50,000 spend and the only person that needed to sign off that money was my boss. Meaning spending below £50,000 was a super quick process for us, and could be turned round in minutes, if we were in the same place. Happy days for the corporate and for the supplier!

Beyond £50,000 and it moved into the second tier. This spend required multiple decision makers and became a lengthier process. I'm not saying this isn't worth it, it just will not be quick because getting multiple sign offs in a busy company takes time, and people can chuck up road blocks to stop the spend, so it's a harder win.

The last one is tier 3. This is for you, if are after the mega buck's contract, I'm talking millions here. Here you will be going into tender process. Probably with at least three cycles and the Purchasing department will be running that show. So the Marketing Director, for example, doesn't have the ability to make the final call.

Be warned, this process may also conclude in a silent Japanese auction between you and the other final listed supplier so that the corporate can get the lowest price possible. Why? Because corporates care about the millions. A lot.

Which leads onto a word of caution...

9. Corporates will make you work

So you've landed a gig with a corporate. Awesome. Go you!

They'll want the help you promised delivered, and on the shortest time scale possible thank you very much. If you have a team you shouldn't need to worry about this. If you don't, don't panic. Just think about how you will cover this, if you are unavailable for a while.

Corporates are used to loads of people that can pick up the slack to get things done on time. They will expect this from you. Make sure you have a plan in place so you can nail the delivery time. Always have a Plan B ready to complete your contracted service. Anticipate what could go wrong and prepare in advance.

They will also expect you to be available on email and phone to accommodate them during business hours. Their big issue is now yours. They are used to being the big fish.

Finally...

10. Once in the Corporate... get around a bit

So you're in, and you are doing a great job. You are Mr./Ms. Popular. You need to capitalize and quick. Make sure you go after multiple relationships within the company whilst your stock is high. Get about a bit.

When you're working with big companies, you don't want to have your entire future resting in the hands of a single person. Why? This people can easily change jobs, leave the company.

And, if you are clever, you can make this corporate career movement lead to a load more business. For example, I had five roles in five years at my last place. Guess what? I took those great suppliers with me everywhere I went. When I changed companies guess what I did? Yep, I took them again.

Also, remember to talk to everyone in the team from the Junior to the Director. Why? Because people climb that corporate ladder. The Junior could be the Director one day, and that's another great opportunity for you.

So there you have it: A decade of inside corporate knowledge crammed into a couple of thousand words. You can, and should, go after your first corporate conquest.

ABOUT THE AUTHORS

Charlie Hutton

C harlie Hutton is a serial entrepreneur, strategic advisor and marketing consultant. He has written extensively about using direct response principles for business-building.

In his training courses, workshops and seminars he teaches small business owners how to dramatically increase leads, prospects and sales while minimizing their marketing expenses.

He's been referred to as a 'Direct Response Aficionado On Steroids,' and since starting his first online business in 1998 aged 16, he hasn't stopped. Charlie's run multiple real-world enterprises - in multiple countries, including a pool company in Vancouver! He's even sold gas and electric over the phone.

It's all played its part in building a vault of marketing and sales knowledge that has led him to be sought out by immensely successful small and mighty business owners for un-canned, impartial expert advice.

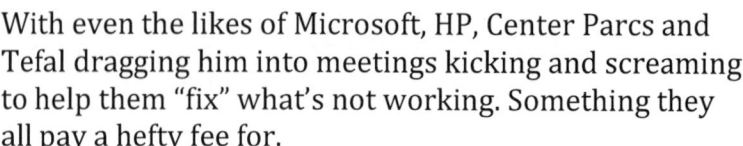

With even the likes of Microsoft, HP, Center Parcs and Tefal dragging him into meetings kicking and screaming to help them "fix" what's not working. Something they all pay a hefty fee for.

As an international speaker to audiences across 75 plus countries, he's shared the stage with countless celebrities, thought leaders, as well as being featured live on air with the BBC. All while his raving 40,000+ fan base on social media lap up his hurricane of ideas, step by step strategies and no nonsense approach to making stuff happen in the real world.

To talk with Charlie direct about his availability for speaking engagements, seminars or corporate training programs, or availability for mastermind meetings or consulting, please email sue@charliehutton.co.uk.

For more information about his books, products and resources join the rapidly expanding community on Facebook at:

https://www.facebook.com/TheOneManEmpire

Emma Hutchinson

E mma Hutchinson comes from the world of big business. A strategic marketer with an uncanny knack to maximise profits by getting existing customers to spend money and do it on a much more frequent basis.

In her career she's been responsible for dealing with budgets in the multiple-millions, plus leading on international marketing campaigns that have seen customers come back and spend at record setting levels. On top of this she's been responsible for replicating this same success with one hand tied behind her back while only being allowed spend pittance (£1.00) to retain a customer.

All in all, her experience with top flight corporates has given her key insights on what really works at scale and, more importantly, what doesn't.

Since leaving her high-paid position in the corporate world she hasn't looked back. Emma now focuses her time and energy on applying and scaling her corporate strategies to a handful of small business clients that wait with baited breath, poised to take action on the next sure-win strategy to come out of her mouth.

In her closed door mastermind meetings she regularly exposes the hidden marketing tricks and psychological sales tactics used by the big guns. She leaves no stone unturned as she breaks downs the numbers for easy implementation and quick wins for every entrepreneur in the room.

To talk with Emma direct about the availability of her mastermind meetings or her consulting please email sue@charliehutton.co.uk.

Don't Forget To Watch The BONUS 4-Part Documentary Series For Free!

Finally *TRANSFORM* Your Business Into "**One Man Empire**" Without Being Held Hostage By An Army of Employees, By Watching This Ground Breaking Documentary Series...

All you have to do is go here now:

www.theonemanempire.com/documentary-fb/

Printed in Great Britain
by Amazon

16595266R00090